D0944529

ISLAND OF WILD HORSES

ISLAND
OF
WILD
HORSES

words by

Jack Denton Scott

photographs by

Ozzie Sweet

G. P. Putnam's Sons   New York

Library of Congress Cataloging in Publication Data
Scott, Jack Denton.
Island of wild horses.
Summary: Presents theories about the history
of the wild horses of Virginia's Assateague Island
and describes their present life and habits.
1. Chincoteague pony—Juvenile literature.
[1. Chincoteague pony. 2. Horses]
I. Sweet, Ozzie. II. Title.
SF315.2.C4S36   636.1'6   78-17380
ISBN 0-399-20648-5

For
MARGARET FRITH,
who had the idea

They came through the dark sea, swimming strongly, heads high, bodies submerged, making for an island that lay suspended and blurred along the misty horizon.

Behind them on the treacherous shoals, hidden by waves cresting and shattering like glass, a Spanish ship was breaking up as seamen attempted to save some of the cargo and their own lives.

Overhead seabirds screeched. Dark clouds raced. A storm rumbled in the distance as the animals clambered out of the bitter Atlantic Ocean. They shook the water from their hides, then gingerly made their way along the white sand beach of the island.

Does this scene accurately describe the dramatic arrival of the rarest and perhaps most famous creatures in the eastern United States—the wild horses of Virginia's Assateague Island? No one knows for sure.

History hedges on exactly how these horses came to their island and offers other theories besides the one just described of a Spanish galleon carrying horses and supplies to Spain's colonies in the New World in the mid-sixteenth century. But this version of the wrecked galleon still persists among the residents of Chincoteague, Assateague's sister island.

As late as 1900, the local fishermen and boatmen associated with the Life Saving Service of the area called the region of Pope's Island and Pope's Bay "Spanish Point" and "Spanish Bar." They claimed then, and they and their descendants still do, that this was the place where the galleon was wrecked and the horses swam ashore.

The island itself is almost as interesting as the horses that roam it today. Although the vanished Indian tribe, the Chincoteagues, is not remembered by present residents of the area, the tribe's name is perpetuated by a town, an island, a bay, and by a national wildlife refuge. All four are on the coast of Virginia, along the Delmarva Peninsula, where three states, Delaware, Maryland and Virginia, meet the Atlantic.

Today, Chincoteague National Wildlife Refuge is one of our most important wildlife preserves, with more than nine thousand acres of beaches, dunes, and marshes. Established in 1943 to save a large portion of coastal wetlands with their valuable and unique wild fauna and flora, the refuge became part of the new Assateague Island National Seashore in 1965.

This refuge, portions of which the wild horses roam, occupies the Virginia section of Assateague Island and about four hundred acres in the Maryland area. The refuge itself is thirteen miles long from north to south, about one and a half miles wide, except at the lower end near Chincoteague town where it widens to nearly three miles.

Backed by high, ocean-made dunes, falling off on the landward
side to freshwater ponds and marshes, some high points of the island of
wild horses contain tall stands of loblolly pines, the only trees of any
height. Others are gnarled, more bush than tree. Plant life is not rich;
growth is mainly wild-grape vines, persimmon, sweet gum, similax,
Virginia creeper, poison ivy, trumpet vines, and myrtle brush.

The horses' grazing grounds are often soggy marshes and salt
meadows; most of their fodder the straggly salt marsh cordgrass and
wiregrass that grows there. Bayberry leaves and berries also provide food.

The horses browse near the shore, nibbling beach grass. Sometimes they walk through the trees in single file, moving on to new grazing grounds, ever in search of sweet green shoots of new grass. They seek shade from the sun in the few copses of pines. They bury muzzles in shallow freshwater pools.

Their seemingly aimless wanderings all have point and purpose—survival. It is not easy on this island. Slender and low in profile, this thirty-seven-mile barrier strand is one link in the disarticulated chain of thirteen islands that hugs the Middle Atlantic coastline, running from the mouth of the Delaware River south along the Carolinas to Georgia. Interplay of wind and sea gave the island of wild horses birth, and even after thousands of years still shapes and nourishes it. The sea carries in the sand, the wind drifts it. Together they form the bulwark shielding the mainland shore from the full force of winter storms.

But the horses aren't on the mainland. They live on the barrier itself and are vulnerable to those seaborne gales. When the skies become dark with storm warnings, the horses attempt to get as far from the sea as they can. The highest point on the island is forty-seven feet above sea level, and the only place the horses can find shelter from hurricanes and nor'-easters is behind sand dunes and in the few pine groves on the barrier. During one hurricane in the sixties, twenty were drowned. Yet, despite storms and harsh environment, the herds live on.

The first reference to the island dates back to 1524 when it was discovered by Giovanni da Verrazzano, but no mention was made of horses.

However, the two hundred years of Spanish exploration and rule that followed Columbus' first voyage to this hemisphere produced famed conquistadors and adventurers such as De Vaca, Ponce de Leon and Cortes. History also records that the Spanish successors to these men sent their soldiers, families, friars, and governors northward. Thus it is possible that a galleon was indeed wrecked off Virginia's coast while attempting to deliver supplies and horses to Spaniards moving north.

But there are other theories on how the horses got to Assateague Island. One goes back to the 1870s, long before the island was widely inhabited and became a town. Some of the earliest settlers claimed that Indians told them that a vessel carrying horses to one of the English colonies was wrecked on the south end of the island. The horses were said to have escaped and the ship's crew rescued by friendly Indians who brought them to the early mainland settlements. The horses, left to themselves on their new island home of Assateague, became wild, and because of hardships endured developed into a singular breed.

There is also a group that maintains that pirates placed the horses on Assateague, "the place across" as the Indians named it. It is believed that pirates often put their horses ashore to graze, then returned them to their ships, fed and ready to continue the journey. This time, according to the "pirate theory," it didn't work. The buccaneers couldn't recapture the horses.

There is yet another theory in which Eastern Shore planters imported horses to the mainland peninsula in the mid-1600s and released some of them on the offshore islands to graze. During three centuries these horses and their descendants became wild and adapted to the island's harsh environment.

But the favored theory perhaps remains the one of the wrecked Spanish galleon. And history does in part support it.

We know that from sixty million years ago until about three thousand years ago, horses of one kind or another, and sometimes several different kinds simultaneously, existed in North America. The best known is the dog-size eohippus of the Eocene period.

But these native species of horse died out, and there were none on this continent until the introduction of horses by the Spanish conquistadors. Darwin, in *On the Origin of Species,* was perplexed over this ancient horse's extinction and concluded that some unknown factors must have been unfavorable to the animals. The reason for his puzzlement was the astounding success in the wild of the modern horses that escaped from the herds brought in by the Spanish colonizers.

When Hernando Cortes landed in Mexico in 1519 with seventeen horses, the animals frightened the Aztec soldiers. But it took only a few encounters with the mounted Spaniards to change the reaction of the Aztecs, and later other tribes, from fear to covetousness.

This was the beginning of horse rustling, usually in the form of raids, first on the Spaniards, then one tribe raiding another. During these raids, often more horses escaped into the wild than were captured by the raiders.

As a result, within two centuries wild horses populated the rangelands of Argentina, Uruguay, southern Brazil, Mexico, the United States, and Canada with the greatest wild horse herds the world has ever known. It has been estimated that at their peak, on the western prairies of the United States alone, in the middle of the last century there roamed as many as five million horses, many of them mustangs that traced their heritage back to Spain.

And what manner of horses can survive on an island for as long as three hundred years, living on thin grass, marsh plants, and leaves? These too are mustangs, physical testament to the theory of the wrecked Spanish galleon.

The mustang of the Plains Indians was originally a "Barb," the result of interbreeding of native Spanish stock with the sleek horses ridden by the Moors from North Africa, whose Barbary horses were descendants of the Arabian horse. Thus, the horse that the Spaniards brought to America had a substantial amount of handsome Arabian blood. The Arabian is the beautiful horse the Bedouin tribesmen of the desert claimed that God had created out of the wind and given to them as their most prized possession.

Most mustangs do not have the clean, sculptured beauty of the Arabian. Their heads, with straight or Roman noses inherited from the Barbary horses of North Africa, are for the most part not as handsome.

The western mustangs are smaller than their ancestors from Spain. Neglect, theft by Indians, roaming wild over the American plains and prairies, plus a certain amount of inbreeding, all contributed toward producing a smaller animal.

This is especially true of the wild horses on the island of Assateague. They are even smaller than the mustangs of the West. But the superb blood of the desert horse, the Arabian, has endowed them with the traits of endurance and a wiry strength which seems to give them the ability to withstand hunger and thirst.

This explains in part how these horses, restricted to an island for so many years, are able to survive. Among them are a few handsome bays, blacks, and sorrels, with heavy, curly manes and long silky tails, clearly reflecting that they are indeed Barbs—Spanish and Arabian—with that delicate beauty of the desert horse clearly visible.

But all of them are also compact and tough, trimmed down by environment and breeding into a species all their own, smaller than the average horse, but much larger than the average pony, averaging five hundred to seven hundred pounds; Assateague Island *horses* whose existence and evolution still baffle historians and horse experts alike.

There are no mass movements of horses on the island, none of the wild scenes of grandeur of large herds racing across open plains, manes flying, heads high, nostrils flaring, the picture we all have of wild western horses running free and unhampered by civilization.

The island horses aren't hampered by civilization, and they do have space, but the collective herd of approximately three hundred never runs in large numbers. A stallion, several mares and foals, yearlings, and often a few older offspring, make up the numerous small bands that move about the island. Bands of eight are not uncommon and groups of more than sixteen rare. (When some larger bands do gather they are the result of numerous families being brought together by favorable grazing conditions.) These remain small bands throughout the year and have favorite grazing and watering places, even special "scratching" trees, where they can be found at certain times of the day.

Each band is ruled by a dominant stallion who guards it vigilantly, for every other stallion that has a band wants to add new mares to it, for the new blood would increase the strength of his own harem. Whether the band is grazing, resting, or drinking at the freshwater ponds, each aggressive male is on constant alert, watching his mares carefully.

But even this vigilance doesn't always keep his band intact. In a surprise raid called a "gathering chase," some crafty stallions, scenting that a mare or mares are in breeding condition, will swoop in and create a minor stampede, startling the band of mares and colts into a gallop.

When the raiding stallion has urged them into a fast pace, no matter what the other stallion, the harem master, attempts, he cannot guard every mare. Quite often the raider is able to cut a mare in heat out of the band and drive her to his.

This fast, skillful operation often is successful because of speed and the element of surprise. It fails on occasion if the stallion that is being raided is stronger, faster, and more alert. If so, he can cut that invading stallion out of the band, do battle, and drive him off defeated and mareless.

[25]

However, every band of galloping horses does not indicate that an attempted abduction of a mare is under way. Frequently bands may even merge briefly for an invigorating gallop across the island. Often this action is sparked by frisky colts who suddenly begin a race along the sandy beach and are joined by the adults in the band. Or sometimes a stallion, seemingly to prove that he is in constant command, will stir his band into a dramatic dash to a change of pasture.

When they are in a gallop, the island horses are sheer poetry of motion. They thrust off the ground with hind limbs and swing the body forward by pivoting over the fore limbs. The resultant jar that is passed to the limbs at every stride by these heavy animals moving at high speeds—which can reach forty miles per hour—is minimized by a beautifully coordinated shock-absorbent arrangement of flexible joints, ligaments, and tendons.

These physical endowments have made the island horse's survival possible. The large head helps it maintain its balance while running or walking. When the horse moves fast, wide nostrils permit an intake of the necessary large flow of air. Eyes are far apart, permitting it to see simultaneously right, left, and behind. Each eye picks up a different sight. The eyes are placed so high that, unlike most other animals, a horse can even look around while grazing. Ears can be pointed in nearly any direction to pick up sound, much like a radar directional finder.

Even the horse's snort has a purpose. It comes from a large empty air pocket inside its nose, enabling it to warm the air inhaled on a cold day. When it snorts, it blows air through the pocket, making an odd hollow sound. It has two kinds of teeth, long sharp front teeth for cutting grass and heavy back molars for chewing. Nose and lips are flexible, soft, and sensitive. Nose and upper lip are used to sort selectively as it grazes, preventing an intake of weeds, sticks, and pebbles. Hay and grain are picked up with the lips. Two-inch whiskers are feelers which judge distance in the dark and act as antennae that help in other ways, for a horse can't see the end of its nose. Sleeping while standing is accomplished by a strong muscle in the neck which supports the heavy head. Elbow joints lock tightly to prevent the legs from buckling.

Social order also aids survival. The island bands have a rule-by-rank society, each horse knowing its place in each band hierarchy, recognizing one another by voice and scent. Each group minimizes aggressive behavior and fighting within the family. They appear to like one another, often nuzzling and rubbing against, even grooming, one another.

The stallion comes first to feed and drink and is the leader in most other situations. Next in rank come the mares, according to size, age, and truculence, then the young. When the band moves, the senior mare is in the lead, and the stallion either brings up the rear or travels at the side of the band. But during the breeding season the stallion moves constantly around the band, keeping it together, challenging and chasing away potential rivals.

Whether the stallion is there or not, mares and their young actually form their own unit and remain together. If the stallion dies or for any reason leaves the band, the normal family existence continues until eventually another stallion may adopt the band. His taking over is accepted as a matter of course by the mares and foals, and there is no disturbance in the rank relationships.

As with most animals, wild or domestic, the spring and summer, when the hours of daylight increase, is the time for mating—for propagating the species. On Assateague Island it also is known as the "time of the stallions," for it is truly their season.

This is the time not only when stallions breed with mares in their band that are in estrus, but the months when young stallions leave their bachelor groups and attempt to prove their virility, trying to form their own bands.

It is a time of contest.

The older stallions must fight off the younger stallions that are searching for mares. These young stallions also do battle with one another to prove superiority and to establish their own harems. If they begin to form their band with a single mare, it is likely that there will be a fight each time a mare is added to the new band.

The young maturing stallions are especially feisty. They strut arrogantly, and sometimes the hair of their manes flares in anger when they near other stallions.

A contest between two stallions is balletlike in its movements and its gracefulness. It may begin with a nudge. Then one stallion slams into the other. They then stand on their hind legs, slowly at first, not fully upright. They flail at each other with their hoofs, much like boxers. Now completely upright, they bite each other. If both are out to prove their mettle, or if there is a young mare nearby ready to be bred, the fight can become vicious. Teeth can tear flesh, sharp hoofs can inflict damage. But the fighting is mainly stylized, with neck-wrestling, biting, and kicking.

Even so, the battles can be fierce and serious, for not only is breeding drive motivating them, but the fight for status is also involved. Superiority, however, is acknowledged. If one stallion clearly is winning, outfighting and outmaneuvering the other, the loser may suddenly drop from his upright fighting stance, wheel, and trot away.

If the fight was over a willing mare, she is quickly herded with the other mares the victorious stallion has collected.

After the spectacle of the battle, the actual mating is almost sedate, a placidly cooperative affair with the other mares completely ignoring the action.

The bred mares remain with the herd until they are about to foal. Only at that point, when they are about ready to give birth, 330 days after the time of mating, will the stallion permit the mare, or mares, to leave the band to have their offspring in a place of their own choosing.

The stallion, however, does not ignore his foaling mares at this time. He keeps the band nearby in case he is needed. There are no predators on Assateague, but both parents nevertheless stay alert for danger.

Inside the mare, the foal has been lying on its back in a filmy sac. Just before birth it turns onto its stomach, its head facing the rear of the mare, so that it will emerge headfirst.

The foal will be pushed down a narrow channel, but before birth a large bubble of water precedes it, helping stretch the channel to make the foal's passage easier.

Finally the foal slides out of the mare (who has been lying on the ground) completely encased in the membranous sac. As the foal is born, it moves, breaking the sac around its head and front feet. Foal and mother are still bound together by the umbilical cord, which nourished the foal during the months before its birth.

Now the mare stands, breaking the cord, freeing the foal, which wiggles out of the membrane which had covered it. The entire action has taken fifteen minutes.

Even before the foal stands, the mother licks off the fetal fluid. She will continue to clean and groom even after it gets on its feet soon after birth. Standing up can take from fifteen minutes to an hour. Sometimes a foal tries a dozen times to get weakly to its feet, then slowly falls back. Immediately after it stands and is able to balance itself, the foal begins to nurse.

The mare continues to groom her foal for some time. The action is not only important in drying her offspring, but also establishes a firm maternal link with her. The mare knows, mainly by sense of smell, that this is her foal (and the foal will also identify its mother by smell) and will refuse to allow any other foal to nurse or even closely approach her.

Mare's milk is rich, so rich that there are desert tribesmen who depend upon it for much of their diet. The little foal, once it has learned to find the teats that release the warm flow of life-giving milk, will nurse during the first week four times an hour.

During the first few days of life the foal will halfheartedly nibble at grass. But it will not begin grazing properly for weeks, and then will carefully imitate the movements of its mother.

The nursing or suckling period will decrease gradually, until it stops altogether when the offspring is about one year old, a time when its mother may be within a few days of giving birth to a new foal. The suckling is sporadic as the foal grows, for grass supplies much of its diet, but it is irresistibly drawn back to its mother for short periods of nursing. The mare is patient, usually permitting it, but if the growing, ungainly youngster interferes with her movements or grazing time she may nuzzle it away from her.

As this is foaling time for the herd, there are other young with mothers nearby. For the most part, during the first ten days there is no association between other mares and foals, although they may be within yards of one another. They will graze as usual, their young beside them, but there is not the usual camaraderie of the band, with the adults sometimes grooming one another or moving together to another grazing area. Each mare with young has a responsibility and an awareness that puts her on constant alert and guard.

It is a rare occurrence, but it has happened that an especially dominant foal-less mare has made a vicious attack on a foal that may have wandered too close. Also, stallions have been known to maul and kill young foals. Thus, until the foals gain strength, speed, and agility, foaling time is a somewhat tense period.

For the first two weeks the bond between mare and foal is close. The two are always together. Sometimes the little horse even lies directly under the mother as she grazes, seeking both the solace of her presence and the shade that her body provides.

The resting periods become shorter as the foal grows. Just before the end of the first month of its life, it begins to notice the other foals in the herd. It will take short exploratory trips away from its mother, not venturing far, but extending the distance a bit each time.

Before, it was hesitant to move near other adults, but each day now it grows bolder and soon walks past other mares and even the stallion to seek the company of other foals. Quite often a pair of foals will stand beside each other as if in silent communication.

At this time, as the spring or summer sun grows stronger and the foals spend more time away from their mothers, you can almost see them grow, day by day. Now is their fun time as they romp and gallop with one another. But it is also more than an enjoyable experience. As they indulge in this exuberance, they are also unknowingly rehearsing with their frolic-mates all the types of skill and behavior that are basic to the life of a wild horse. These play tactics and experiences reinforce and add to those received from the mothers. The foals are also learning to use the code of communication that serves to order the existence of their species. It is believed that horses have a quick eye for slight muscular movements and changes in postures of their companions and communicate many of their feelings by signaling in some subliminal manner.

Mothers and foals recognize and respond to one another's sounds. Certain loud neighs or whinnies may alarm the entire band and alert it for flight. But horse experts believe that in the main, so far as communications between individuals are concerned, visual signals are more important than sounds. So perhaps the two foals standing silently beside each other are indeed in some sort of youthful and mysterious equine conversation.

As the weeks pass, the playful foals begin to indulge in mock-fights. Soon, because of precocious sexual behavior, such as clumsy mounting, the males and females begin to separate and seek one another's company. But they still remain with the family band ruled by the stallion.

The young males leave these family groups between the ages of one to three. They are not driven away by the stallion as potential rivals, as they are on friendly terms with the master of their band. They leave to consort with other males of their own age, forming bachelor bands of as many as fifteen. It is a loose-rank order with no specific male dominating. From time to time males will break away from these bands to form their own family units with any available females they can acquire.

Young females leave the family band at the time of their first estrus, when they are about fifteen months old. This early heat period is seldom fertile, but its scent is strong and attractive to the roving young males in the bachelor herd. They are too numerous to be driven off by the family stallion, who often becomes exhausted in his efforts to chase them away. Finally, one young male out of perhaps a dozen persistent suitors succeeds in abducting the young female in heat, driving her away from her family group.

The attachment between the young female and her male abductor is rarely permanent. She spends about a year with the stallion or one family group after another until she becomes mature and settles down with the stallion she happens to be with at the time. If he already has gathered a family group, she becomes a member of that harem. If he is a bachelor, then she becomes the nucleus of a new band.

There are terms for horses through these various stages of development. From a *foal,* the youngster, after weaning, at about six months becomes a *colt,* if a male; a *filly,* if a female. At a year of age, both colts and fillies become *yearlings.* When they are four years old, colts are called *stallions* and fillies become *mares.*

Horses live longer than cats and dogs, but not as long as humans. Few survive beyond the age of thirty.

When that brown-and-white youngster with the blaze on his forehead becomes a colt and begins to forage for himself, he comes face to face with his bleak island world, its marshes and sparse grass, its chill winds off the ocean, its sudden rain squalls, its lashing storms. And its hordes of biting insects.

He has physical weapons against the horseflies and mosquitoes, a skin that he can wiggle at will to shake the insect off, mane and tail that act as flyswatters. He also can vigorously shake his head to dislodge them.

But in the summer, when the insects are at their worst, he will roll on the beach to brush them off and ease the pain of their bites. Or swim in the guts of freshwater, even in the ocean, to gain relief.

This wetland world of the horses of Assateague is shared with other wild creatures that also receive its mantle of protection offered by all U. S. wildlife refuges.

Many kinds of egrets visit the island, as do the gooselike brants. Three hundred varieties of wild birds come to this island every year, some during the migrating periods, others as breeding and nesting birds, some just as seasonal visitors.

Some, such as the unique cattle egrets, spend much of their time with the herds, eating the insects flushed by the horses as they graze.

It was the presence of these wild birds, especially the wildfowl, ducks, swans, and geese, that brought yet another hazard for the wild horses to face. Howling storms, inadequate food, harsh environment, weren't enough. Politics arrived to plague them.

The horses' new troubles started in 1943 when Assateague Island was designated a national wildlife refuge.

Conflict began almost immediately between the people of the town of Chincoteague, who view the horses as a wildlife asset, and the federal fish and wildlife service, which is in charge of the island.

The horses and the wild birds had coexisted on the island for centuries, but that fact was discounted by the federal agency. The fish and wildlife officials built dikes and discs to protect the government-built wildfowl ponds. To further protect the dikes from being trampled by the horses, fences were erected, restricting the horses' movements and grazing to a low, marshy, insect-infested portion of the nine-thousand-acre island.

As a consequence, the horses' range was reduced to five percent of the total land area they once had roamed. This not only greatly curtailed grazing, but the fencing prevented them from reaching the ocean surf where they had habitually obtained relief from the vast swarms of mosquitoes and biting flies that pester them during the summer months.

The space restriction to the low-lying swampy areas was a direct cause of twenty-two horses drowning during the hurricane in 1962.

But the wild horses of Assateague are luckier than the beleaguered mustangs of the West that are being shot, illegally, and sold for dogfood, pushed off their ranges by the cattlemen and stockmen who have strong lobbies in Washington.

Eventually, the people themselves saved the wild horses of Assateague. This untenable political situation did, however, persist to the horses' detriment until 1965. That year the national park service began to operate on the island, opening the beaches and a large portion of the island to the public.

Parks are for people, and the people, who came from many states, liked to view the wild horses. The horses were appreciated far more than the wildfowl.

So the park service removed many fences and permitted the horses to roam freely on the dunes in the large area that was under U. S. jurisdiction. As a result, the horses, although not permitted freedom of the entire island, now have space. But that space becomes more precious each year.

Exotic animals from Japan also share the island with the wild horses. In 1923, a Boy Scout troop released several sika deer on the island. Smaller and shyer than the native white-tailed deer, the sika have done so well that periodically they must be weeded out so the whole herd will not be weakened.

Many naturalists and biologists do not approve of this kind of action, with humans as controlling factor, the weeder-outer, the decision-maker as to what is to live and what is to die (or be relocated).

On the western ranges and prairies it may be good natural logic for biologists to explain that it is normal for wild horse populations to experience peaks and crashes, without the interference of man. Naturalists claim that studies of rabbits, deer, and other species prove that animal populations are regulated by density and weather cycles. (Hardly anywhere anymore is predation, long supposed to be the major factor in population control, thought to be important, as we have upset the balance of nature by wiping out many of these predatory animals.) When food, water, and birth sites become scarce, herd vitality wanes, fewer young are born, and the weak are eliminated. This leaves the strong with more to share among themselves.

This thinking, however, isn't valid with the island sika deer or horses. Range and food are permanently restricted. The island can sustain only a certain number of horses. Going beyond that limit would spell disaster for the herd, for overpopulation would weaken not just a few, but all of the animals.

This is the logic of the guardians of the wild horses of Assateague.

For more than fifty years the eleven herds of wild horses of Assateague have been the wards of the Chincoteague Volunteer Fire Company. Respecting their "wildness" and freedom, the firemen do not "manage" the horses. If winters are especially severe, they will bring hay to the island and chop holes in the iced-over freshwater ponds. This is accomplished with four-wheel-drive vehicles and fire axes. If the weather is so bad that even rugged trucks and Jeeps cannot move, a helicopter is hired to drop food. Other than this, the horses are for the most part left to live their life as they please.

But they are fortunate to have the firemen looking out for them. During one hard winter the firemen drove to the island to feed the horses and found a mare lying in the snow, apparently frozen to death. As they were about to leave her, one of the men thought he saw her breathing. They watched carefully. Even though frozen almost solid, she was still alive.

Somehow the firemen managed to get her into a truck, drove her to the firehouse, thawed her out, and nursed her to health. They discovered that she had been bred and would have a foal, and took care of her until her foal was born and mother and offspring were doing well. The firemen named the foal Icicle. Mare and foal were returned to their island. Icicle became the all-time favorite of the men, and still roams Assateague.

Since 1924 the firemen have also controlled overpopulation in a unique way that has become a tradition. During the last Wednesday and Thursday in July they hold their annual Firemen's Carnival and Auction.

About a week before the carnival, the firemen, mounted on regular riding horses, go to Assateague to round up all the wild horses and drive them into corrals.

Although the mares usually give little trouble in the corrals, stallions often become aggressive. They snort and buck, and rear up from the herd, their long necks reaching serpentlike above the backs of the rest of the herd.

Early Wednesday morning, the day of the carnival, the horses are released and driven to Assateague Channel. It is at low tide, and the swim is an easy one for the horses, who all swim well. The firemen and their horses follow on a raft. Ashore, the horses are driven through the main street of Chincoteague to the carnival grounds, where huge crowds, often as many as fifty thousand, await the wild horses and the auction, both of which have become famed nationwide.

Young colts and fillies, usually about forty horses each year, are sold to the highest bidders. All money received is used to buy equipment for the fire department and winter fodder for the horses.

When the auction is over, the horses are driven once again to the channel and swim, unescorted, back to Assateague.

As they leave the water and trot along the beach of their island, the horses of Assateague are perhaps reliving that long-ago experience of their Spanish ancestors.

Each July, history dramatically repeats itself as the herds swim back to the safety of the island of wild horses.